The World Is a Woman You Love

The World Is a Woman You Love

First Edition
Published on 2/21/2020

copyright © Hala Numan 2020

cover art photographed and designed by
Hala Numan

ISBN: 978-1-654427-07-8

ACKNOWLEDGMENTS

MAMA.

MAMA.

MAMA.

BABA.

THE WORLD IS A WOMAN YOU LOVE

HALA NUMAN

SACRED

The World Is a Woman You Love

you tried to run away from yourself
and you found me.
you can't run from me.

i am the face that you see when you
close your eyes.

⊙ **open your eyes** ⊙

with palms like rain
his touch
was ritual
purification.

⟪ **holy places** ⟫

love is war   **SIDE A**

she is called
to administer prayers

in a religion
where everyone
is on their knees.

⊙ **humility** ⊙

love is war   SIDE B

love is a war
in which no one is the victor.
each single person devotes themselves
to a cause
crucified with palms wide open.
to be on our knees
willingly bleeding out on a field.
a field where strawberries
are rotten and violent.

and we take no god, no hope.
we return wounded,
acting as though we
have not just been to war the night before.

❨ **pride** ❩

lone-li-ness is lack of one-li-ness.

if you know yourself
you become a threat
to those who tried to
make you forget who you are.

☾ **remembrance** ☽

my remembrance is my amulet
i wear it on my tongue daily
there is no more rust.

only water.

⊙ **God is still on The Throne** ⊙

that is how we go
to people sometimes.

empty

wishing to be filled.
instead
let us sit.

let those come to us
who wish to spill
over.

《 **LOA** 》

"Why be ashamed to know you are beautiful?"
Because it is not mine to know.
I did not Mold my beauty.
I have only grown in the right direction.

◉ **Sunflower** ◉

you will eventually die of thirst
if you don't submit to the desert.

《 **Universal Law** 》

when the world is shooting missiles like fire
He is teaching you to be still like water.

don't aim.
flow.

⊙ **battlefield** ⊙

What is Crying?

Crying is mourning
the small wars
in your bones

the aches and the fevers
that crack
at the joint.

Your hip rolls
and into another woman you
become.

When you wail
you are communicating
with the haunting ghosts of
your past.

Your wailing and beating
chest
forges anew
and your tears

your tears

flower into petals that grow
on your lips.

Once again,

having given birth to
yourself.
You become a wild oak tree
a field of petals
waiting for rainfall again.

don't ask people if they are hungry.
those of nobility
will not say they are.

so feed those who always
seem to be full.

☾ sacred fruit ☽

infinity   SIDE A

it's about rituals
not routines.

rituals awaken you.
routines deepen your slumber.

⊙ **you don't know**
you're dreaming until
you wake up ⊙

infinity

SIDE B

a rolex will still tell you
that you're running out of time.

☽ a cage is still
a cage
even if it's gold. ☾

when someone wants to leave you
let them.

when someone wants to love you
let them.

⊙ **ego** ⊙

If you must speak, speak with modesty.
If you must eat, eat with humility.
If you must die, die with dignity.

Conversations of Eroticism

*"How do you explain to someone
the geometry perfected in creation?
The frequencies,
the colors,
the nine months,
the sun,
the ocean,
the mountains. How?"*

"Not by begging."

"Then how?"

"Show them this."

This world is a way station.

When you are on a long arduous journey,
you are bound to struggle through cold
brutal nights. On those nights, finding
warmth is of priority.

Stopping in at a friend's to stay warm,
drink tea and depart once again.
A love that keeps the heat alive in our hearts.

That is this world.
We are dying to stay warm.
Until we are dead cold.

We are always seeking warmth until one day
we are no longer here.
Only elsewhere.

Maybe on another rock. Another journey,
seeking someone else's warmth.

You are only a traveler.

BE.

YOURSELF.

ROOTS

Roots are a web of interconnectivity.

A solid silk of strong abstracts.

Fulfilling the desire of the tree to grow upward.

The roots establish the intention of the tree, wholly

WOMAN SAYS:
let me come inside.

MAN SAYS:
Let me
come
inside.

everything eventually finds it's way home.

⊙ **paradise** ⊙

i will scorch the earth looking for you.
that is how grand my love is.

☾ **persephone** ☽

I wanted to teach someone how to love.
So that's exactly what I did.

I walked away from the world
and belonged to myself.

she burns.
that is how she lights the path for others.

why reach around in the dark
when you're holding the light?

we all stand knee deep
in the same pools of struggle,
wishing for life lines from the kings above,
never knowing that rescue is done alone.

"*i told her everything that she wanted to hear.*
i spoke fluidly like water entering the long-stemmed
body of a rose."

⊙ **man-boy** ⊙

What is strength?

Strength is the ability to stretch without breaking.

Love is the frantic search for wholeness
in a world that only divides.

⊙ **Albert** ⊙

hiatus

"how are you going to shame someone for the same practices you engage in? hypocrisy is a disturbing form of self-loathing."

When in doubt, act.
Acting breeds confidence.
Confidence builds self-esteem.
Love arrives shortly thereafter.

Letter to Lover

May we wisen up with the
wine of scholarship
to be students of love. to be a teacher
who raises his beloved to new heights
that remain ancient
with no ruin.

To engage and enlighten, to laugh
and in-lighten. To learn to give
and be patient.
To reserve my sharpened words
for the battlefield of scholarship and
not the home-dwelling
of lovers.

Gentleness and kisses on the cheek.
Playfulness that of children
who have yet to meet
the Chieftain of Mischief
and Deceit.
Of children eating
sunflower seeds

on cement blocks;
staircases of
neighborhood boredom.

The innocence found
in lying on a rooftop
to witness the salt
and pepper droplets
stuck in our heavenly sky. To imagine
dragons and fairies in
the constellated fire
held in our above.

To learn Divine love.
A spiritual quest of
heightened station. To
remind each other of
the travelers that we are
traversing this pyramid
of capital-isms.
This is my intention.

To love deeply, wounds
of past aside and
to be loved in return

not for my sake but
for the sake that we
may become great in
one another's gentle
escapes
into the laughter
found in the napes
of necks.

To be loved
by the beloved
of my Beloved.

This way, we will
taste life. Oh sweet
honey, I await your
becoming one with
my mouth, my body, my belly.

meet me in the space beyond place.

EXHALE

to breathe in,

means to breathe out.

if you hold your breath out of fear

you will suffocate on that which was meant to give you life.

you must first let go.

my favorite memories
were in your car
when i could look over
and see you my love…

like a piercing
your body will reject that
which does not fit you
that which is not made for you.

so if they tell you no.
know that if they lived in you
it would have made your blood rust.

instead say thank you.

and pull the salt from the shelf.
mix with warm water
and melt.

☾ **sanitized** ☽

suck in your cheeks.
draw in your breath.

let me nuzzle into your lungs.
be the smoke to your relief
in an anxious world.

you are a past life
victorian unpolished silver
a distant village
rust on my feet from traveling loveless.

ghost-man,
i have forgiven you.

you may pass now.

☾ **a haunting** ☽

Draw your words on my breath
so that every time I inhale,
I become full with you.

father, where are you?

you are at home
in war.

with half a heart
and a cigarette for lips.

you said you recently quit.
so why is it that when you speak
all i see is smoke and mirrors?

she held us in her mouth
for too long
kept quiet for too long
now
when she smiles
we spill out,
so she doesn't smile much anymore.

⊙ **the reason why** ⊙

you held me at the tip of your tongue.
blew out when you wanted me gone.
blew in when you wanted me home.
i can't say i didn't go with the wind.
i did.

☾ **loved without a trace** ☽

rx   **SIDE A**

anger is pain on fire.

⊙ **smoke** ⊙

rx   **SIDE B**

douse with water.
let pain rise to surface.
speak to it.

☾ **self-medicate** ☽

love as much as you breathe.

words hang off lips
dripping down in allegiance
to the original promise:

      to be woman
      to remain mute.

the morning comes again
to have to look him in the eye

but he's blind
and she has been eating the same meal
for 30 years
and starving.

Every day something happened that I
wanted to share with him.

Laughing at our inside jokes
alone.
It was hard explaining them to people.
They never laughed. They looked at me
with pain in their eyes.

To them I was a woman writhing in pain
holding on to a hope of return.
I was nothing more than a sheer curtain
in the wind.
Blowing.

you let go
every time you breathe.

letting go
is in your nature.

☾ **how to**
release back to
the wave pt. 1 ☽

his chest rises
like the sun.
every breath
a small war.

she loved this fisherman
but he threw her back
into the sea

catching his breath instead.

⊙ **back to**

the wave pt. 2 ⊙

FRUIT

the fruit is the dream of

the root made manifest.

sweet
cherries
in your cheeks
hiding
savoring the moment
before swallowing seedlings that
expand in your throat
and flower wildly
in your belly.
filling until another day.

another tongue.

caught between
wakefulness
and desire
for sweet honey,
sweet honey.

⊙ **the lovers** ⊙

whenever he calls your name
you find a little bit of the East
running through his voice.

crimson flowing from between
his cherry lips.
a breath of iron-will.

he imagines you swimming nude.
inviting you to float on the back of his wings.
butterfly.

you are the city-scape, architected might
lighting Fortuna's wheel alight.
destiny molds anew
in the middle of the night.
and with the flap of his wings,
you rise to the sky
taking flight.

☾ **Aquarian Man** ☽

☉ How many times do you think he
has written a text without pressing send? ☉

☾ How many times do you think she
has written a text without pressing send? ☽

i was in my own world
disassembling myself
and then i found you.

《 **love note** 》

falling in love   SIDE A

loving you was an accident.

⊙ **trippin'** ⊙

falling in love

SIDE B

loving you was an accident.
you happened to be there
that tuesday night.

when no one was looking up
from their phone
except for you.

you were loving the stars.

☾ **universalist** ☽

we are nothing but stars in intermission.

pour some pleasure in my cup.
stranded on a spinning rock.
waiting for the next great record
to change the way we love.

and how i taste this night
twice.
valerian root for the insomniacs
one hot, one iced.
pinky dipped in orion's belt
sugar crystals hang from your lips.
how i taste this night
twice.

pink knows no limits
fold you inside, keep you safe.
you swim nude
skin-clothed
it's warm inside.
and how you taste this night
twice.

《 **religion** 》

maybe feeling whole
is piecing together
the jagged edges of each other
so that we are not so sharp anymore.

⊙ **love note 2** ⊙

men, you are beautiful.

❨ **words you don't hear often** ❩

you count the cellulite dimples
on the back of my thigh
leaving your fingerprint impressions
like the craters on the moon.

building boats to discover
the continents on my back
while tracing the soliloquies you hear
down the stream of my spine.

qamar is the name you gave me.
you know my subtle insecurities
and you turn them into pools
of prayer.

⊙ **royal jelly** ⊙

GOLD

fixed.

unaffected

by air.

the only current.

you want nirvana
but you're on a diet
not trying to die yet.

create waves.
ride them to the bank.

⊙ **universal tongue** ⊙

see reflection in river.
drink.

⊙ **love-self** ⊙

all I've ever wanted was a place to breathe
where no one told me to do it quietly.

☾ **warring women** ☽

All born to die.
The unknown guarantee.
Look in my eyes and tell me
This isn't the most thrilled you've ever been.

⊙ **Super Traveler** ⊙

if you've learned anything
from me all this time
it's that Life is the final act
in God's master play
and you are the after party.

((**love note 3**))

What does it mean to be free?

If not to make art
that creates
a reality
more real
than our obligations
to a rumbling law and order.

I am not complicated.
I am complex
full of contradictions.
Fears that arise as fevers
that break in the moments of loving you.
A man I'm always on the verge
of finally meeting.

☾ **Blowing on Stars** ☽

tonight

Why is it that you choose to call after
the people that have their backs
turned? You imagine a world in which
they are yours and only yours. You
spend hour on dreadful hour in their
presence feeling constrained. Whether
or not to tell them how you feel. You
exist in the plentitude of their smile
and you know you can give them the
world if they opened their palm so you
can graze from their affection.

Constantly stuck in a standstill hoping
that you don't have to tell them even
once more how you feel. You never
wrote them poetry because you were
scared that they'd actually fall in love
with you. And you know. You know the
minute they realize your flaws, they
won't love you flaws and all. You'll be
disparaged and banished and
recalculated into dust.

You give them eyes of lust, admiration, echoing over and again how your infatuation has driven you into a deep binge on ethereal sadness and cosmic laws of attraction. You hope that one day they'll actually take the time to recognize the godliness in your eyes and crown you with adoration.

But it's all for nothing. In the end, you chose to call after someone that had their back turned. Not because you hurt them, but because you never caught their attention to begin with. That. That is even more painful than losing a love. That.

That is losing your creative imagination to a disheartening reality. All the lies you fed yourself and you never became full.

Instead, starved and incurable.

A moving target
is never vulnerable.
Stay light.
Dance around your enemy.
Those who are inflexible
are quick to retire.

⊙ **Rebellion** ⊙

you cannot quench their thirst
if your well is empty.

《 **The Source** 》

when the night brings forth shudders
from relationships left broken
piece together a blanket,
a vase and add live flowers.
become alive with the sanctity of May.
spread the heat over your feeble bones
and become strengthened with
your desire to love and be loved.

the mountainous regions of your body
have no space for the finite.
you are boundless and never circumstantial.
you belong in all places.

1. reminder to the lovers

you are sacred.
and it is your right
to set up obstacles
you feel they must
overcome in order
to prove that
they love you.

2. reminder to the vulnerable

protect yourself.
not everyone has
your best interest
at heart.
not everyone wants
you to shine.
not everyone is
proud of your
accomplishments.

3. reminder to the forgiving ones

you have the right to walk away
when what you are being offered
is not enough for you.

4. reminder to the loners

as we float in the biodome
of the gut of this universe
and Venus looks on longingly
at us

we notice for a moment that
everything we will ever
amount to
are the trees
that populate this earth

that fill our eyes with
Beauty
and our bodies with
Breath.

we are stardust
that landed on Earth.

SEEDS

some see dirt.

others see potential.

READ
THIS
EVERY
DAY

do not
become deafened
by their doubt.
re-emerge.

They kick.
Not to fight off their own shoes.
They kick to fight their way through
a system.
Kick to swim through a canal
that was designed to push them out.

《 **Homeland** 》

Your potential
frightens them at the base of their spine.

Their fear of losing
means you've already won.

⊙ **Glass-House** ⊙

You made me pregnant
With dreams.
Then you gave me shackles and told me
"Be free."

☾ **Oppression** ☽

you don't fit in.
because you were meant to

stand out.

heartbreak is the ego

c   a   k   n
   r   c   i   g

☾ **shadow-self** ☽

you used to interrupt me.
to hear the dentistry of your own voice.
drilling holes through our sorry love story.

i found the way out of a hell you called home.

◉ **eviction notice** ◉

he continues to show up
at the door
every time i close it.
he knocks the way
a seed bursts
through the ceiling.
misfit.

thwarting me?
you can't see yourself.

the hours evade you.
your time has run out.
and i grew.

☾ P(L)OTTING ☽

when pain is life
you find beauty in
the in-between places
the crevices in the scar.

the steaming tea
with cardamom pods
sweetened with rock sugar.

on a morning when
siege is the rising sun.

⊙ **war-zone** ⊙

a woman under
fire by the
public
simply
fuels her.
throw the stones.
start the furnace.

she is stuck between two earths.
to drown?
or to swim?

⊙ **mermaid** ⊙

I didn't need permission
to fall in love with you.
Night makes the distance feel short.

When I sleep
I travel to you in my dreams.
It is a quick embrace:
a glitch in the furnace of the sun.

❨ **Lucid Dreamer** ❩

loss:

heavy like a swollen tongue.
11 dollars and 73 cents to your name.
a used lighter.
3am visit on 92 degree-weather night.
petals for hands.
wood planks for teeth.

sitting next to someone on a hill
as the sun sets
and feeling them fall away and out
of love.

to be:
split between deities.
split like parents.
split seeking solitude.

our faces are glorious.
lit up.
not from enlightenment.
we are far from illumination.
but from cracked phone screens
blocking our Vision.

we can't see anything.
barely our own reflection.

☾ **3rd i** ☽

those diamond eyes
looking right through me.
i am not scared anymore
of falling
straight into the middle of your heart.

☉ **love note 4** ☉

After opening up to you completely
You left me like an open wound.

I slept too much
trying to dream of your face.

I packed my bags
to travel from you.
And somehow I ended up at your door
with broken keys

☾ **broken dreams.** ☽

waking up
to the words
I love you

is to know peace
in times of war.

⊙ **revolution** ⊙

"why are you standing in the dark?"
have you noticed?
people have never asked
why are you standing in the light.

the natural inclination for a human
is to be attracted to light.

we learn to dwell in the dark
when the darkness within
doesn't make us nervous anymore.

☾ **"why are you standing in the dark?"** ☽

choose hope.
every
time.

FLOWER

the height of Beauty

lasts but a moment.

When the moon is full
it does not question its lineage.
it's right to shine for a night.

Disappearing
it is not disappointed.
It passes through phases to fullness.
Like you.

So when you wake up in the middle of the night
hungry for more
sweating from nightmares filled with bills
and unresponsive lovers
know that it may be dark now
but it is only because you are new.

⊙ **Mansions of The Moon** ⊙

your soul is scented like blossoms
fragrant even more in a sleepless night.

❨ boys don't have insomnia ❩

the cake.

the cake sits beautifully
mounted on crystal.
her eyes sparkle at the thought

someone will give her a cake one day.
a cake to reach down the back of her throat
and tickle her sweet cravings for love.

no one told her,
her teeth would decay.

***

the consummation later that night
solidified the contract.
never to be nullified
even if she left.

he was only there in stolen moments
her whole life, a theft.

"Let's hold hands
next time around
it'll be different
I promise.
I'll be more honest."

☾ **nostalgia, famine, grace** ☽

she isn't lovely.
she is lonely.

captive.
in her own story.

she is the magician
but the only thing
she can't do is
disappear.

i still can't believe i think of you.
i used to wake up looking for you.
now, i sleep to find you.

《 **bed** 》

A dream.
Somewhere there's a dream
where we are not.

We are a glimmer on a pond as the sun sets.
A glimmer in the Eye of God.

⊙ **Divine Dream** ⊙

you insist on shaving your beard
in the winter
but watering it in the summer.
you rebel in silent ways.

☾ **metamorphosis** ☽

delirium   SIDE A

being in love with someone
who isn't blind
but can't see you.

☉ **stop-motion** ☉

delirium   SIDE B

you blinded me
so i never noticed when you left.

((**dust**))

Love is a salve
which escapes death.

For moments
we are flowers
in a field of wheat.

i know you have to go
take some summertime with you
turn the leaf over
and find me

☾ **fallen.** ☽

we are all dying.
that is the curse.
so love what kills you.
that is the cure.

⊙ **i love you** ⊙

roseblades cut the inside of
my cheeks
as i search for fragrance
with my tongue.

《 **Hope** 》

the child
and the elder
walk at the same speed.

⊙ **Irony** ⊙

when your skin begins to fold
it is because parts of you
are falling in love with each other.
needing to be closer.
and isn't that lovely.

《 **Aging** 》

i found myself without you.
now
i am finding my way back.

⊙ **becoming** ⊙

if i had it my way
we wouldn't live together until love
left the sheets dry.
until sunrise wouldn't shine.
i would leave the party before the last person.
i wouldn't wait until the last raindrop of
a thunderstorm.
i would leave before nostalgia builds
a home in our hearts.

☽ **jeux d'enfants** ☾

you are the rose's bloom, honey

TREES

the seasons change

but the tree is the same.

my body
pines
vines
twists
and
turns
reaching
stretching
for the sun
but winter
always comes.

you
fall
in and out
of old scars.

leaves
falling
in and out
of love with summer.

me
falling
in and out
of love with you.

❨ **seasons** ❩

Trees are always grinding their feet into the
world, into the dirt. They show their teeth to
the stars. They shower us with shadow.
They grow. Their bare bark exposed and
hardened to their conditions.

They've harnessed their inescapable fate:
To be still. Quiet. Unassuming.
But they know everything. They've seen it all.
Yet they can't speak about it. Or complain.
They only breathe. Trees breathe.
Don't you know? Just like us. They grind.
They agonizingly hustle.
Growing. Still. In silence.

⊙ **The Perennial Hustle** ⊙

he who does not know
your value
will always suffer
the loss.

❨ *"stay with me"* ❩

she reveals herself
slowly

you are alone with her
every time she speaks

warm handfulls
of pleasure
petaled lips
floral breaths

reading you stories
from her imagination

she is the day
you are the night

she is all you can believe in
when all hope is broken.

shadows and outlines of your beard
scratch the surface of my chaffed lips
and grow into the branches
and leaves of my spring.

☾ **winter** ☽

conversations with a blind man:

when sadness was the sea,
you taught me how to swim.

I stretch toward you
the way she flowers toward the sun
but you break my branches instead.

"have you ever seen a grown man cry?
his beard becomes thicker somehow."

i slipped
into my dreams
and watched them become my nightmares.

watched the man i love.
scatter.

⊙ **ashes** ⊙

He says:
"be silent and listen"
and to that i say:

what are the ways to flee from sea monsters
when we live on an island of anxiety?

i hope we don't lose our minds
from creditors
loaning us love
and lining our pockets
with lint.

i see the ring of armor around your eyes
and i know
that you have fought yourself for so long
that you have forgotten what side you're on.

❀ all selfie, no Self ❀

start
speaking
as if you
already
have
the attention
of the
whole
Universe.

it's time to turn the page of your own story.

sacred roots

exhale trees   exhale fruit

sacred seeds   gold seeds

flower fruit   flower trees

gold roots   sacred gold

fruit trees   roots seeds

exhale flower